It CAN'T Be TRUE!

POO!

Written by Andrea Mills and Ben Morgan
Senior editor Ben Morgan
Design Laura Gardner Design Studio
Illustrators Adam Benton, Peter Bull, Dynamo Ltd,
Stuart Jackson-Carter, Jon@kja-artists.com, Arran Lewis,
Andrew Pagram (Beehive Illustration), Gus Scott

Jacket design Akiko Kato
Jacket editor Emma Dawson
Jacket design development manager Sophia MTT

Producer (pre-production) Jacqueline Street-Elkayam
Production controller Meskerem Berhane

Managing art editor Owen Peyton Jones
Managing editor Lisa Gillespie
Publisher Andrew Macintyre
Art director Karen Self
Associate publishing director Liz Wheeler
Design director Phil Ormerod
Publishing director Jonathan Metcalf

First published in Great Britain in 2019 by
Dorling Kindersley Limited
80 Strand, London, WC2R 0RL

10 9 8 7 6 5 4 3 2 1
001–314300–October/2019

A CIP catalogue record for this book
is available from the British Library.

ISBN: 978-0-2413-8145-8

Printed in China

A WORLD OF IDEAS:
SEE ALL THERE IS TO KNOW

www.dk.com

CONTENTS

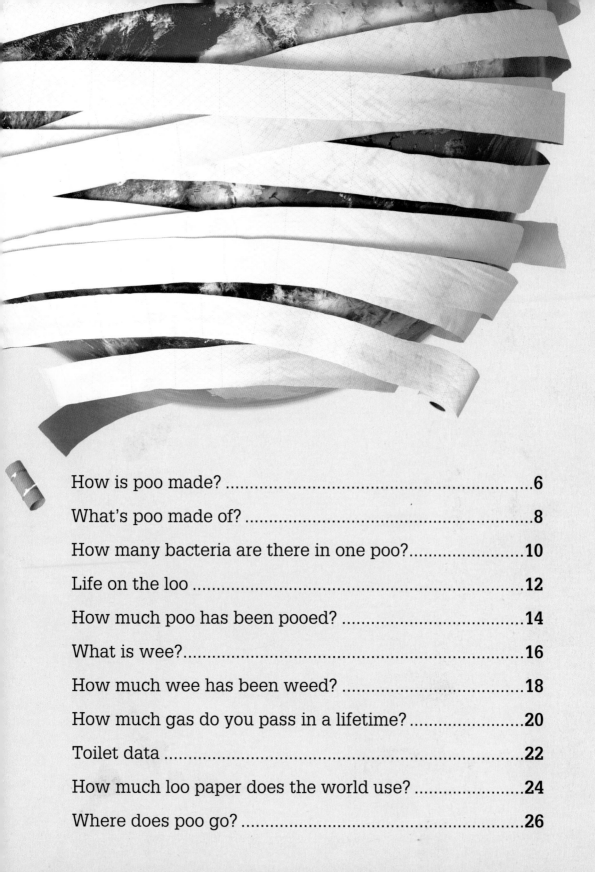

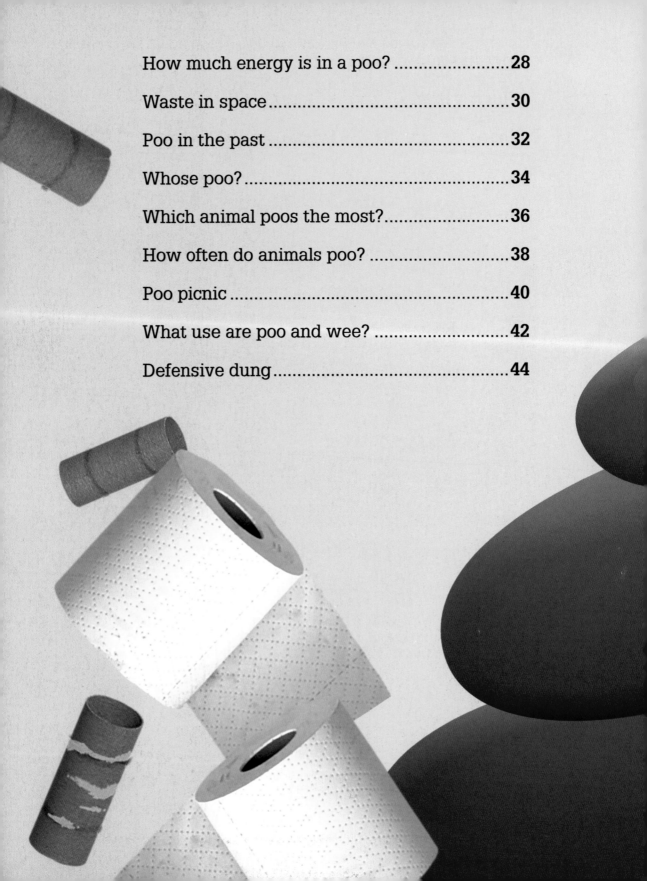

How is poo made?

Poo is made by your body's **digestive system** – a set of organs that work together to break down food into molecules your body can absorb.

1. **Your tongue and teeth** mash food into a pulp, and chemicals in your saliva (spit) start to break it down.

2. **When you swallow,** mouthfuls of food are squeezed down a long tube (the oesophagus) to your stomach.

FAST FACTS

24–48 hours

It takes 24–48 hours for your digestive system to turn a meal into a poo.

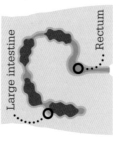

Large intestine

Rectum

Your intestines have muscles that squeeze food and poo to push them along. When they do this, you hear your belly rumbling.

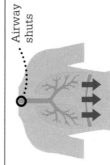

Airway shuts

Pushing out a poo uses lots of muscles, including those in your chest! Your chest muscles squeeze your lungs, but the airway that lets air escape shuts. This makes your lungs push down on your intestine.

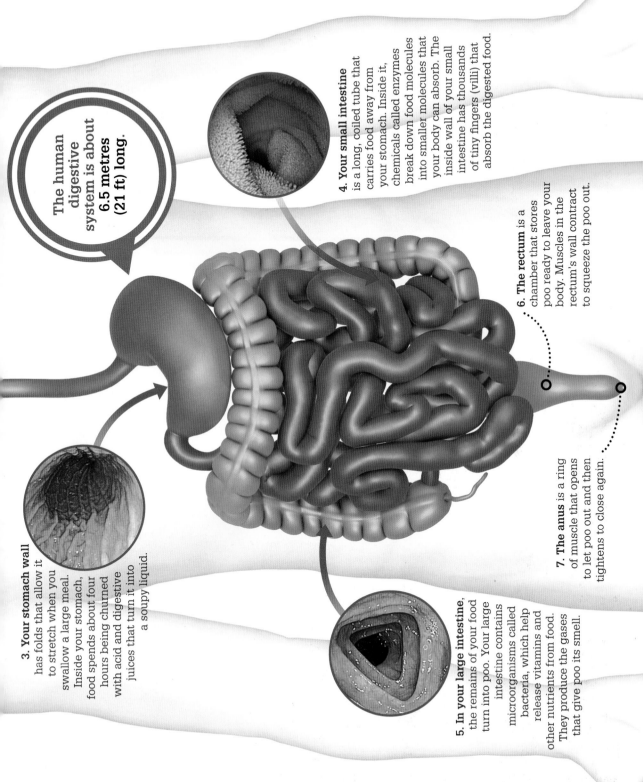

The human digestive system is about **6.5 metres (21 ft) long.**

4. Your small intestine is a long, coiled tube that carries food away from your stomach. Inside it, chemicals called enzymes break down food molecules into smaller molecules that your body can absorb. The inside wall of your small intestine has thousands of tiny fingers (villi) that absorb the digested food.

3. Your stomach wall has folds that allow it to stretch when you swallow a large meal. Inside your stomach, food spends about four hours being churned with acid and digestive juices that turn it into a soupy liquid.

5. In your large intestine, the remains of your food turn into poo. Your large intestine contains microorganisms called bacteria, which help release vitamins and other nutrients from food. They produce the gases that give poo its smell.

6. The rectum is a chamber that stores poo ready to leave your body. Muscles in the rectum's wall contract to squeeze the poo out.

7. The anus is a ring of muscle that opens to let poo out and then tightens to close again.

What's poo made of?

Poo isn't just undigested food. About **half its weight** consists of **microscopic organisms** called bacteria. They come from your microbiome – an ecosystem of organisms living in and on your body.

DIETARY FIBRE

Dietary fibre helps keep you healthy by feeding friendly bacteria in your large intestine and by making poo bulkier and therefore easier to push along. Foods rich in fibre include beans, wholewheat, and vegetables such as corn.

Live bacteria make up about a quarter of poo. Poo is a living substance, with more than 1,000 species of bacteria. It also contains smaller numbers of viruses, fungi, and microorganisms called protists and archaea.

An average **human poo** contains about 250 microscopic particles of **plastic**.

Inorganic compounds such as sodium and calcium salts make up about 7% of poo. They come from your food, your digestive juices, and from the layer of slimy mucus that coats the insides of your intestines.

Fibre from plant foods makes up about 6% of poo. Our bodies can't digest fibre, but some of the bacteria in the human microbiome can.

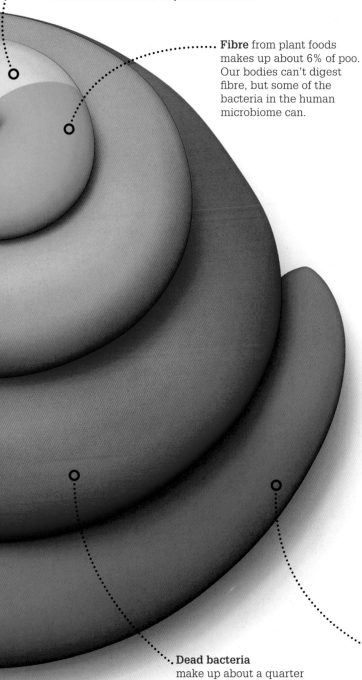

Dead bacteria make up about a quarter of poo. Their remains are food for the trillions of bacteria that are still alive.

FAST FACTS

Cow dung contains masses of microbes but little plant fibre. That's because cows have special stomachs housing bacteria and archaea that digest the fibre in grass.

Rabbit droppings have lots of bacteria and lots of plant fibre. Unlike cows, rabbits can't digest fibre in their stomachs and instead rely on microbes living in their large intestine.

Bird droppings are packed with bacteria from their large intestine. Birds mix their poo and wee together, which is why their droppings have black (poo) and white (wee) patches.

Water makes up just over one-third of the weight of poo. Your intestines also secrete a slippery, watery fluid called mucus onto the surface of poo to help it slide along.

How many **bacteria** are there in **one poo?**

A poo of average size **contains a mind-boggling** 10,000,000,000,000 (ten trillion) bacteria, as well as billions of other microorganisms.

POO VIRUSES

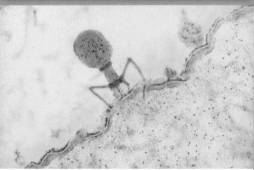

Even smaller than the bacteria in poo are viruses — the smallest life forms on Earth. One level teaspoon of poo contains up to 5 billion viruses. Most are bacteriophages — viruses that attack bacteria. Built like tiny spacecraft, complete with landing legs, they land on bacteria and inject their own genes to take over the cell.

There are 50 times more bacteria in one poo than there are stars in the Milky Way galaxy.

The Milky Way galaxy that we live in contains 200 billion stars, but a poo contains 10 trillion bacteria. If you counted all the bacteria in a poo at a rate of one a second, it would take over 300,000 years to count them all.

FAST FACTS

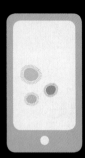

Poo bacteria are so tiny and numerous that they get everywhere. Tests reveal that 1 in 6 phones have live poo bacteria on the screen.

Scientists call poo bacteria faecal bacteria. Some kinds of faecal bacteria spread dangerous diseases — which is why you should always wash your hands thoroughly after visiting the loo.

Escherichia coli and Shigella kill 600,000 people a year.

Vibrio cholerae kills 100,000 people a year.

Salmonella typhii kills 200,000 people a year.

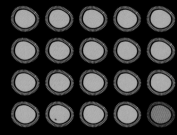

Fewer than 1 in 20 faecal bacteria are harmful. The rest help keep you healthy. We call these good guys your gut flora.

Life on **the loo**

Most people poo **once a day**, which adds up to about 29,000 number twos in a lifetime. If it takes you **five minutes** each time, you'll spend **100 days of your life** pooing.

📊 FAST FACTS

Poo production varies wildly across the animal kindgom. This is how much poo various animals do per day.

Mouse: 0.6 g (0.02 oz) a day (the weight of one blueberry)

Chicken: 21 g (0.7 oz) a day (the weight of 4 cherries)

Rabbit: 60 g (2 oz) a day (the weight of 5 strawberries)

Dog: 140 g (5 oz) a day (the weight of 1 apple)

Pig: 500 g (17 oz) a day (the weight of 3 bananas)

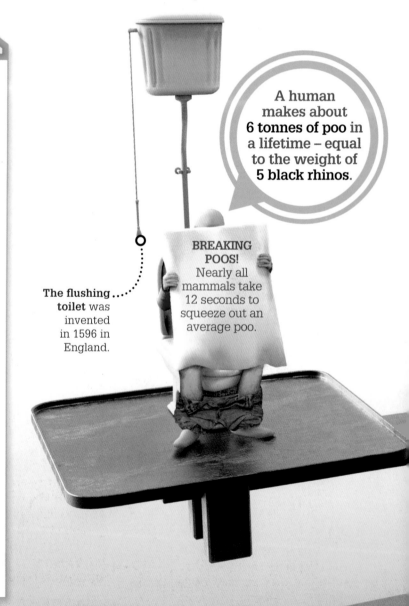

A human makes about **6 tonnes of poo** in a lifetime – equal to the weight of **5 black rhinos**.

The flushing toilet was invented in 1596 in England.

BREAKING POOS! Nearly all mammals take 12 seconds to squeeze out an average poo.

Poo size varies a lot from person to person, but the average adult human produces about 200 g (7 oz) a day. Over an average 79-year lifespan, that amounts to the weight of five black rhinos. By contrast, an African elephant can drop up to 220 kg (485 lbs) a day – up to 1,000 times more than a human.

All the rhinos in the same area poo in a single communal heap called a dung midden.

Rhinos may be built like tanks, but they can achieve 55 km/h (34 mph) in a sprint, which is 50% faster than the world's top Olympic sprinter.

DOGGIE DIRECTION

Scientists have found that dogs prefer to face north when pooing. This may be because dogs use poo pit stops to recalibrate their internal compass, which they use to find their way around.

How much **poo** has been **pooed?**

Over the course of history, the **human race has pooed** a grand total of about 200 billion tonnes of poo.

11 km (7 miles)

3.4 km (2.1 miles)

📊 FAST FACTS

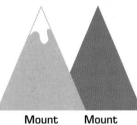

Mount Everest   Mount Poo

The total weight of all human poo in history is about the same as the weight of Mount Everest from base camp to summit.

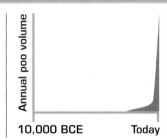

Annual poo volume

10,000 BCE   Today

The quantity of poo the world makes has risen dramatically along with population growth. Every year, we poo more in a year than ever before.

22 km (14 miles)

All the poo in history would make a single log as long and wide as **Manhattan Island** in New York, USA.

Big cities like New York City in the USA have to cope with an ever increasing volume of poo as their populations grow. All over the world, cities are expanding and upgrading their sewers to manage the never-ending flow of waste.

POO LENGTH

If all the poos that humans have ever produced were joined into a single unbroken poo of average width, it would be 130 billion km (81 billion miles) long, which is long enough to stretch to the Sun and back more than 400 times.

What is **wee?**

Wee is a mix of water your body doesn't need and **thousands of waste chemicals** produced by your body's cells. It's made by two organs, called kidneys, that continually filter and clean your blood.

📊 FAST FACTS

Kidney.....

Bladder.

Every minute, a quarter of the blood in your body passes through your kidneys. They filter out waste chemicals and water that your body doesn't need. The resulting liquid drains into a storage organ called the bladder.

  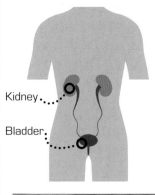

Size of an empty bladder

Half full

Size of a full bladder

Your bladder expands like a balloon as it fills up with wee. An empty bladder is about the size of a plum, but a full bladder is as big as a grapefruit. The bladder's wall is made of muscle that squeezes to make the wee shoot out.

Scientists have identified more than **3,000 waste chemicals** in human wee.

0.2 % other chemicals

0.2 % creatinine

0.3 % potassium

0.4 % sodium

0.7 % chloride
Sodium and chloride
make up common salt.

3.2 % urea
This is the main waste
chemical in wee and
comes from the
breakdown of
proteins.

URINE X-RAY

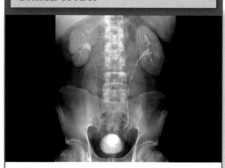

Doctors can check your kidneys are working properly by giving you a special kind of X-ray that makes wee visible. First the doctor injects your blood with a chemical called iodine, which shows up on X-rays. A few minutes later, your kidneys will have removed the iodine from your blood, making your kidneys and bladder visible on an X-ray.

90–98 % water

Human wee is an incredibly complicated liquid, with a chemical make-up that changes by the hour. However, the vast majority of it is water. If you drink too much water, your blood becomes dilute and your kidneys respond by taking more water out of it. So as well as getting rid of wastes, your kidneys keep your body's water level in perfect balance all the time.

How much **wee** has been **weed?**

The human race has weed a mind-boggling **1,400 cubic kilometres** (336 cubic miles) of wee throughout the whole of human history.

Enough wee has been weed to keep North America's **Niagara Falls** flowing for **18.5 years**.

KANGAROO RAT

Desert animals like the kangaroo rat wee very little because they can't afford to waste any water. The kangaroo rat never drinks water. Instead, its body creates water chemically by breaking down food molecules in its cells, which produces water and carbon dioxide as waste products.

Niagara Falls on the US-Canada border is the most powerful waterfall in North America. Every second, 2.4 million litres (630,000 gallons) of water gushes over the towering cliff.

FAST FACTS

On average, the human body produces 1.4 litres (3 pints) of wee every day. That's enough to fill two bathtubs in a year.

The colour of wee depends on how much water you take in. The less water, the darker your wee. The colour comes from the chemical urochrome, produced when old blood cells are recycled.

How much **gas** do you **pass** in a lifetime?

The bacteria in your intestines **produce a lot of gas**, and it has to go somewhere. Every day, an average 700 ml (1.5 pints) of **gas erupts** from the human anus. Over a lifetime, you pass about 20,000 litres (5,000 gallons) of gas.

You pass enough gas in your life to fill 2,000 party balloons.

FAST FACTS

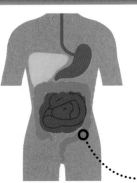

Farts are made by bacteria in your large intestine. They use a process called fermentation to break down fibre in food, producing gases as waste products.

Large intestine

Foods rich in fibre

Foods that make you fart more are good for you because they include lots of fibre. Although these foods increase the volume of farts, they don't make them smelly. The smell comes from foods rich in sulphur, such as meat and dairy foods.

Most people fart about 8–12 times a day, but some people toot hundreds of times. A typical fart consists mostly of odourless gases including hydrogen, carbon dioxide, and nitrogen. Smells come from tiny quantities of sulphur gases, which make up less than 1 per cent of a fart.

ANIMALS THAT DON'T FART

Not every kind of animal farts. Sloths make gas in their intestine, but the gas is absorbed by their blood and breathed out. Birds have never been seen farting. This might be because they digest food so quickly that gases cannot build up.

Toilet data

FLUSH TOILET

A tank called a cistern stores water for flushing.

Bowl

Double bend

Water trapped by bendy outlet

Poo

Modern flush toilets were invented more than 200 years ago. Before then, toilets were too smelly to keep in the home. A simple but ingenious invention solved the problem: a **double bend** in the outlet pipe traps water, blocking smells from the sewer. In many flushing loos, the outlet pipe also works as a siphon — a pipe that sucks water when it's full. Siphonic toilets suck waste out of the bowl after flushing and then make a noisy gurgle before the bowl refills with water again.

1. Before flushing, the bowl is full of water, forming an odour seal.

Water rushes out of the cistern.

Water fills the outlet pipe.

2. When you flush, water surges into the bowl, washing out the waste. The outlet pipe fills, triggering the siphon effect.

Water is sucked out of the bowl until air enters the outlet.

3. The siphon effect sucks water out of the bowl until air enters the outlet pipe. The air stops the siphon effect and causes a gurgling sound. The bowl then refills with water.

BIDET TOILET

Warm water jet

Control panel

The latest **electronic toilets** make loo paper unnecessary. They shoot a precisely aimed jet of warm water at the user, followed by a blast of air from a blow dryer. Called bidet toilets, some also feature electrically warmed seats and loudspeakers that play music or flushing sounds to mask embarrassing body noises.

INCINERATOR

In remote places without sewers, poo can't be flushed away. Incinerating toilets solve the problem by **burning poo** in a built-in oven and turning it into ash. Because the bowl isn't flushed with water, it's lined with fresh paper each time you use it.

Chimney

Paper-lined bowl

Inlet pushes poo into oven

Oven

PIT LATRINE

Around **1.8 billion of the world's people** use a large hole in the ground instead of a flushing loo connected to a sewer. This type of toilet is called a pit latrine. If the pit is large and deep enough, it lasts for years before a new one has to be dug.

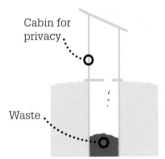

Cabin for privacy

Waste

COMPOST TOILET

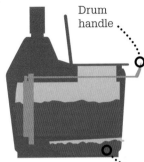

Drum handle

A composting toilet turns poo into compost. Waste is stored in a rotating drum that must be turned several times a week. When it's more than half full, contents are released into a finishing drawer, where they spend a month turning into compost.

Finishing drawer

SUCTION TOILET

To save on water, toilets in planes use **powerful suction** to empty loos. The suction is created by pumps or by vents that connect the waste storage tank to the exterior, where the air pressure is much lower than inside the plane.

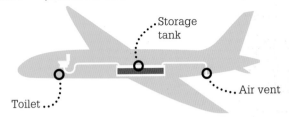

Storage tank

Toilet

Air vent

FREEZER TOILET

A **freezer toilet** freezes waste until it can be disposed of. Poo drops into a bucket lined with a biodegradable bag and is chilled to subzero temperatures by refrigerant gases, just like food in a freezer.

Poo

Freezer

How much **loo paper** does the world use?

The Vikings used snow, the Romans used a sponge on a stick, and sailors used a wet rope. Today, **most people** in the Western world use **loo paper** for personal hygiene.

> **Every hour, the world uses enough loo paper to wrap around the planet 14 times.**

Toilet tissue was invented in China more than 1,400 years ago, but it took a long time to catch on. Mass-produced brands, marketed as "splinter free", became widespread in Europe and North America only a century ago. Today, paper is most popular in colder parts of the world, while people in hot countries often use water for washing and paper just for drying, if at all.

FAST FACTS

Every day, the world uses about 270,000 trees' worth of loo paper. Fortunately, nearly all of it comes from recycled paper or sustainable pulpwood plantations — trees grown for making paper.

In one year, the average loo paper user gets through 28 loo rolls. The total length of 28 rolls is about twice the height of the Eiffel Tower in France.

FATBERGS

Loo paper is made of weak paper fibres that separate when wet, helping it break down. Wet wipes, in contrast, are made with plastic fibres that don't break down. They build up with cooking fat in sewers, forming fatbergs that have to be dug out. Heavy rain makes sewers overflow, washing wet wipe fibres into rivers and oceans, harming wildlife.

Where does poo go?

1. Flushing sends poo down a vertical drainpipe and into a horizontal pipe in the ground (a sewer). All the dirty water from your home – from baths, showers, sinks, washing machines, and dishwashers – goes into the sewer too.

Drainpipe

Sewer

2. The sewer from your home joins other sewers, flowing into bigger and bigger pipes. These run for miles across town, with a hidden river of dirty water gushing through them. Eventually they reach a sewage plant.

3. At the sewage plant, the wastewater flows through a grid of metal bars called a screen. This filters out things that shouldn't have been flushed down the drain – rags, sticks, and even plastic packets.

Screen

New York City has **11,900 km (7,400 miles) of** sewers – enough to stretch a quarter of the way round Earth.

4. Next the dirty water enters a long tank called a grit chamber, which slows it down. This makes small bits of sand and grit washed into the sewers by rain sink to the bottom.

When you flush the loo, you send your waste on a **long and strange journey** that makes dirty water clean again.

6. Dirty water now flows into an aeration tank, where millions of air bubbles pass through it. Oxygen from the air stimulates the growth of microbes that kill dangerous poo bacteria in the water.

7. A second clarifier tank holds the water for several hours. Microorganisms in the water settle on the bottom, forming more sludge. Some of the water flows back to the aeration tank, supplying fresh microbes. The remaining water, now much clearer, leaves for the next stage.

5. The water is pumped up into the middle of a circular tank called a primary clarifier. Here, it moves so slowly that tiny particles of poo fall to the bottom of the tank and settle as sludge. Rotating scrapers push the sludge into a pit for collection.

Sludge scraper ......

Sludge tanker ......

8. A disinfection tank kills any remaining bacteria by treating the water with either chlorine chemicals or ultraviolet light.

Ultraviolet lights ......

10. Clean water flows back into a river. Some sewage plants also filter this water through sand beds or wetlands as an extra precaution.

9. Sludge from the clarifier tanks is heated to kill bacteria and then goes into a digester tank, where harmless bacteria feed on the organic matter and break it down. The leftover solids are burned, buried, or used as fertilizer on farmland.

How much energy is in a poo?

The human body has to be regularly **recharged with energy** from food, but our bodies don't extract all the energy from our meals – about **10–15 per cent escapes in poo**.

POO POWER

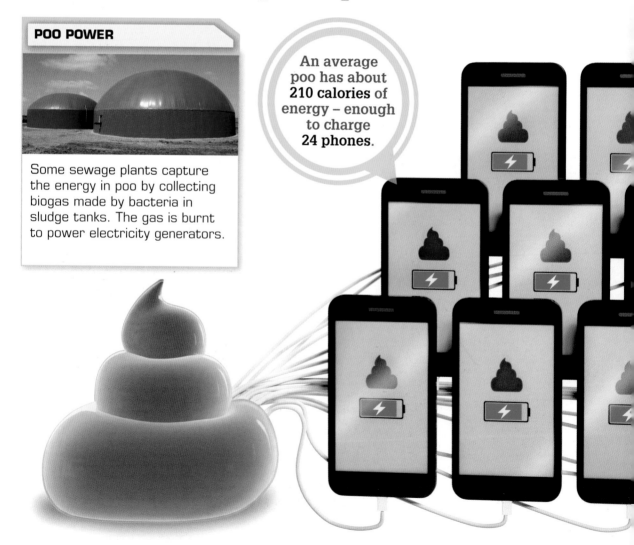

Some sewage plants capture the energy in poo by collecting biogas made by bacteria in sludge tanks. The gas is burnt to power electricity generators.

An average poo has about **210 calories** of energy – enough to charge **24 phones**.

FAST FACTS

Every day, the world's population poos out an incredible 10,000 terajoules of energy. That's about as much as 150 World War II atom bombs.

If all the poo in the world was collected and used to make biogas, it could supply enough renewable energy to provide 138 million households with electricity.

An average poo has as many calories of energy as two bananas. If all that energy could be captured, it could charge 24 smartphones or power 45 LED light bulbs for one hour.

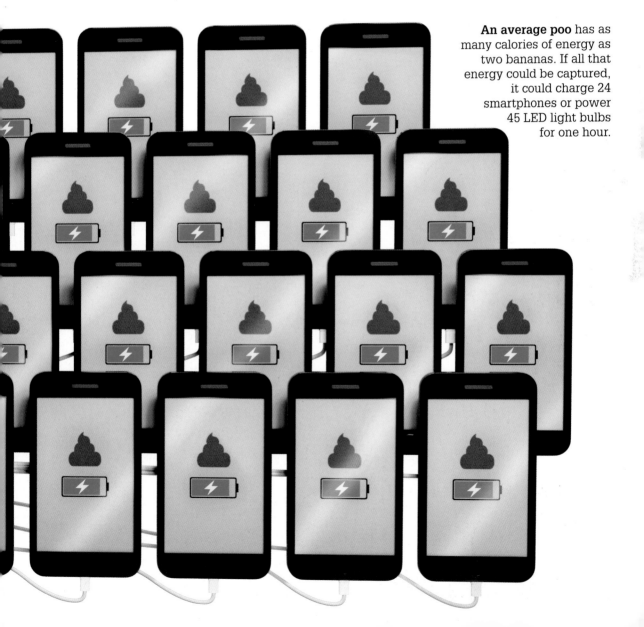

Waste in space

Rockets are not the only thing **blasting off in space**. When nature calls, **astronauts** on board the International Space Station use special loos to hoover up **floating faeces** and **urine globules**.

Before spacewalks, astronauts adjust their diet to reduce the need to poo inside the spacesuit.

SPACE STATION TOILET

Using the loo in space can be messy and takes up to an hour, including cleaning up. Flushing with water is impossible, so the toilet uses suction to pull wastes into it. The yellow funnel is used for wee. To poo, the user must sit very precisely on a hole under the seat while floating weightlessly. Perfect aim is essential.

During a year in space, an astronaut will drink an average 730 litres (193 gallons) of wee and sweat recycled into water.

Spacewalks (trips outside the space station) can last several hours, so astronauts must wear a special pair of shorts, called a maximum absorbency garment, under the spacesuit. This contains a powdery chemical that can absorb 300 times its own weight in wee.

About 3–4 times a year, space station poo burns up in the atmosphere as a **shooting star.**

 FAST FACTS

The International Space Station recycles urine into water, but poo is stored and later ejected into space.

Toilet

Poo bag
The astronaut poos into a plastic bag in the seat. The bag is tied shut and pushed into the storage container under the seat.

Storage
When full, storage containers are stowed with other trash in a cargo supply craft attached to the space station.

Destruction
Released from the space station, the cargo supply craft burns up as it reenters Earth's atmosphere.

If astronauts ever embark on the long trip to Mars, they may need to find clever ways of recycling their poo.

Fertilizer
Poo could be used as a fertilizer to grow plants, providing a source of fresh food.

Space food
Another idea is to turn poo into an edible paste, like yeast extract, by growing microbes in it.

Radiation shield
Waste bags full of poo could be used to line the walls of spacecraft, creating a protective radiation shield.

Poo in the past

Before **flushing loos and loo paper** were invented, people found all sorts of inventive ways to **dispose of their deposits**.

In ancient Rome, visitors gathered in public toilets to catch up on gossip or talk business – while they did their business. They sat together on long stone benches with holes over a sewer that washed poo into the river.

Instead of toilet paper, the Romans used a **wet sponge on a stick**, dipped in vinegar.

Toilet

Medieval castles often had toilets that extended from an outer wall, with a seat over a hole so that poo and wee fell straight in the moat. Fashionable ladies sometimes stored their dresses here because the smell kept clothes moths at bay.

English kings employed a "groom of the stool" – a servant whose duties included changing the monarch's underwear, wiping the royal bottom, and cleaning the portable toilet, which was known as a close stool.

Medieval ships didn't have bathrooms. Sailors relieved themselves over the bow (front), either by leaning over the side or by perching over openings in the deck. They used a soggy rope dangling in the water to wipe themselves afterwards.

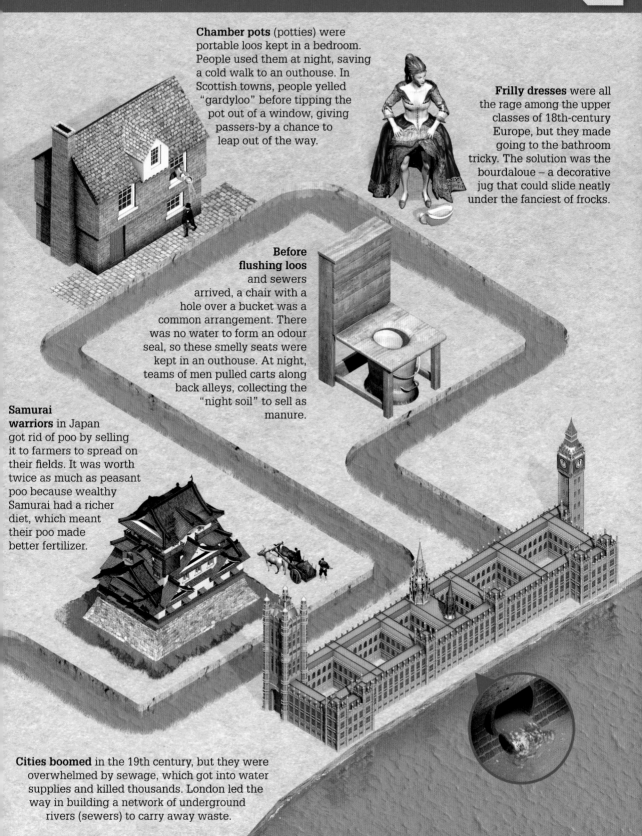

Chamber pots (potties) were portable loos kept in a bedroom. People used them at night, saving a cold walk to an outhouse. In Scottish towns, people yelled "gardyloo" before tipping the pot out of a window, giving passers-by a chance to leap out of the way.

Frilly dresses were all the rage among the upper classes of 18th-century Europe, but they made going to the bathroom tricky. The solution was the bourdaloue – a decorative jug that could slide neatly under the fanciest of frocks.

Before flushing loos and sewers arrived, a chair with a hole over a bucket was a common arrangement. There was no water to form an odour seal, so these smelly seats were kept in an outhouse. At night, teams of men pulled carts along back alleys, collecting the "night soil" to sell as manure.

Samurai warriors in Japan got rid of poo by selling it to farmers to spread on their fields. It was worth twice as much as peasant poo because wealthy Samurai had a richer diet, which meant their poo made better fertilizer.

Cities boomed in the 19th century, but they were overwhelmed by sewage, which got into water supplies and killed thousands. London led the way in building a network of underground rivers (sewers) to carry away waste.

Whose **poo?**

Leopard
Foul-smelling and sticky. Colour varies from pale brown to much darker after a blood-rich meal. May contain fragments of bone, fur, or feathers.

Hippopotamus
Shapeless dollops and splats, very fibrous. Hippos spin their tail like an electric fan when defecating, breaking up the dung into a spray of debris.

Hyena
Brownish when fresh but turning white as it dries, due to large quantities of bone. Hyenas are scavengers and use bone-crushing jaws to devour the remains of carcasses.

Elephant poo is packed with fibrous plant material.

Camel
Very dry, egg-shaped pellets that burn easily. To reduce their need for water, camels have long intestines that extract nearly all the moisture from droppings.

Giraffe
Small, dark pellets, blunt at one end and pointed at the other. They emerge as clumps but scatter on hitting the ground due to the long drop from the point of exit.

Mouse
Tiny dark brown sausages, smaller than rice grains and with pointed ends. Squidgy when fresh but brittle when dry.

Black ant
Heaps of tiny, dust-like droppings stored in a special chamber in the nest. Other waste, such as dead ants and food debris, is dumped in a separate heap.

Elephant
Large, moist clods full of straw and half-digested plant matter. Soft and warm when fresh, with a pleasant aroma, but turns hard and crumbly on drying.

Sausages or pellets? Fragrant or foul? Squidgy or firm? **Animal poos** come in an **amazing range** of shapes, sizes, textures, colours, and smells.

Rhino
Large, roughly cylindrical masses that feel soft and fibrous due to large amounts of plant matter. Often stamped on and kicked apart by the rhino spreading its scent.

Llama
Small, dry pellets, often clumped together. Llamas absorb most of the water from their poo because they live in dry places.

Wild boar
Strong-smelling, lumpy sausage made of pellets pressed together in the rectum. Texture varies from fudge-like to fibrous.

Beaver
Packed with wood chips and sawdust, with a rough, fibrous texture. May resemble small coconuts, but oval in shape.

Chimpanzee
Similar to human poo but softer and paler. Strong aroma. May contain undigested seeds, which chimps pick out and eat.

Fox
Small fudge-like sausage, often with a twisted point. Foul, overpowering odour and maddeningly sticky. Colour varies from black to brown or grey.

Bird
Irregular splat consisting of a slimy white fluid and darker, semisolid patches.

Goat
Smooth, glossy pellets that exit the body in a sausage-shaped cluster but often break apart and scatter on landing. Similar to sheep droppings.

Guinea pig
Smooth, sausage-shaped pellets, glossy and dark when fresh but turning paler brown as they dry.

Rabbit
Pea-sized pellets that feel soft and fibrous. At night, rabbits produce edible droppings that they eat directly from the anus.

Cow
A runny porridge that forms a flat pancake on hitting the ground. Contains little plant fibre thanks to the cow's efficient digestive system. Crust dries brown but reveals a vibrant greenish interior when broken.

Which animal **poos** the most?

The **African elephant** opens its bowels up to **20 times a day**, dumping a grand total of 220 kg (485 lbs) of dung.

A week's worth of elephant poo weighs up to 1.5 tonnes – as much as 25 people.

POO PICKERS

Elephant poo contains lots of undigested leftovers, such as seeds, which other animals pick out to eat. It also contains so much water that some people squeeze it to get a drink.

The largest land animal on Earth, the African elephant eats up to 90 kg (200 lb) of food a day – a weight greater than an average human.

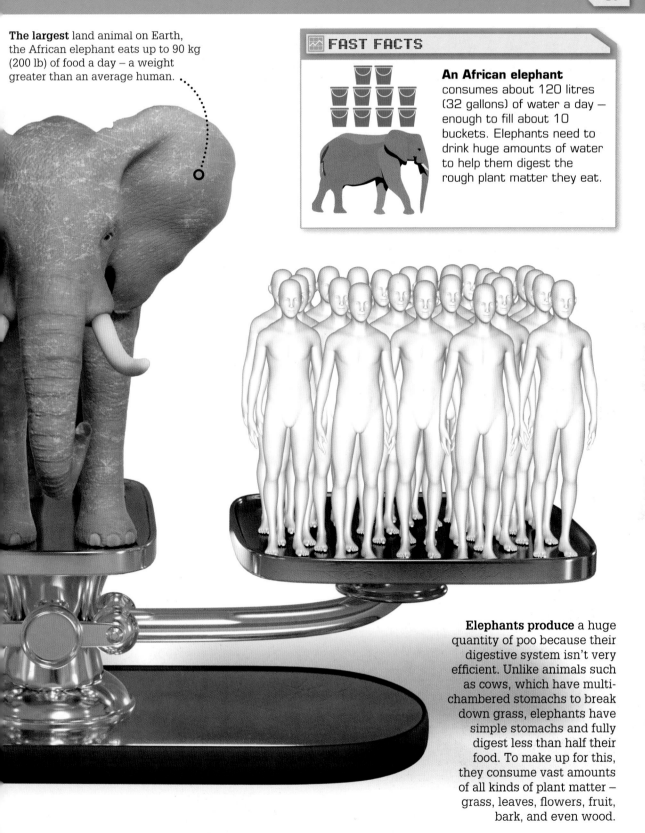

FAST FACTS

An African elephant consumes about 120 litres (32 gallons) of water a day — enough to fill about 10 buckets. Elephants need to drink huge amounts of water to help them digest the rough plant matter they eat.

Elephants produce a huge quantity of poo because their digestive system isn't very efficient. Unlike animals such as cows, which have multi-chambered stomachs to break down grass, elephants have simple stomachs and fully digest less than half their food. To make up for this, they consume vast amounts of all kinds of plant matter – grass, leaves, flowers, fruit, bark, and even wood.

How **often** do animals poo?

Mayfly

Never
Adult mayflies have no mouths and don't eat.

Snake

From once a day to once a year

Large snakes can survive for more than a year without eating anything. So there's nothing to poo.

Sloth

Once
a week

Sloths save up so much dung between toilet trips that they can lose a third of their body weight when pooing.

Cat

Once
a day

Cats are carnivores and produce much less poo than plant eaters. One poo a day is enough.

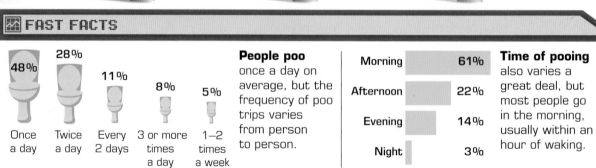

📊 FAST FACTS

48%	**28%**	**11%**	**8%**	**5%**
Once a day	Twice a day	Every 2 days	3 or more times a day	1–2 times a week

People poo once a day on average, but the frequency of poo trips varies from person to person.

Morning	61%
Afternoon	22%
Evening	14%
Night	3%

Time of pooing also varies a great deal, but most people go in the morning, usually within an hour of waking.

Humans poo about once a day, but other members of the animal kingdom visit the bathroom more often or less often than us. **How frequently they go** depends mainly on what they eat.

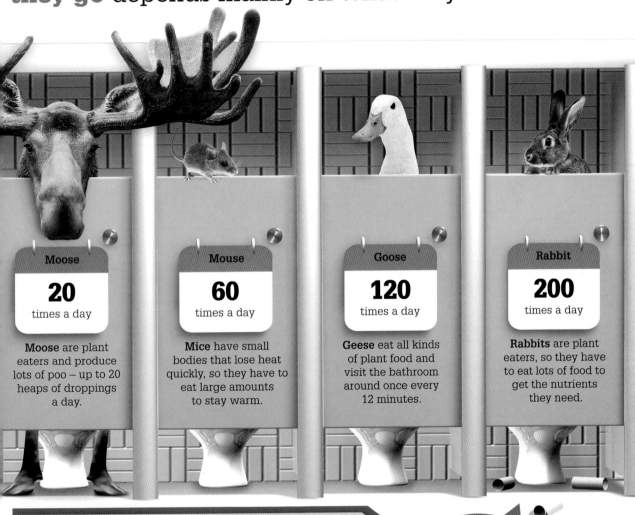

Moose

20

times a day

Moose are plant eaters and produce lots of poo – up to 20 heaps of droppings a day.

Mouse

60

times a day

Mice have small bodies that lose heat quickly, so they have to eat large amounts to stay warm.

Goose

120

times a day

Geese eat all kinds of plant food and visit the bathroom around once every 12 minutes.

Rabbit

200

times a day

Rabbits are plant eaters, so they have to eat lots of food to get the nutrients they need.

FAECAL PLUGS

During their winter hibernation, black bears may have to last seven months without a loo trip. To guard against leaks, their bottoms become blocked by a faecal plug made of dried poo and swallowed hair.

Animals that poo pellets poo the most often – up to **500 times a day**.

Poo picnic

Good news: **humans don't have to eat poo**! This is because our diet contains all the **nutrients** we need. However, many animals love nothing more than tucking in to some **fresh faeces** – including their own.

THE SWEETEST POO

Sap-sucking insects such as aphids poo out so much sugar from their diet of plant sap that their liquid droppings are irresistible to ants. In return for this liquid lunch, ants guard the aphids from predators.

The **practice of eating poo is known as coprophagy**.

Rabbits and guinea pigs eat special droppings containing partially digested food. The soft pellets, called cecotropes, help them absorb extra protein and vitamins.

About one in six dogs eats poo, but exactly why is a mystery. Wild dogs and wolves eat their pups' poo and lick the pups' bottoms to clean them.

The capybara is a giant South American rodent that produces two types of poo: hard pellets, which they discard, and soft ones, which they eat. The soft stuff contains nutrients released by bacteria in the capybara's intestine.

Egyptian vultures get the yellow pigment that colours their face by eating cow dung. This makes them more appealing to mates.

Butterflies get salt by sucking liquid from fresh poo – even human poo!

Baby hippos, koalas, and elephants swallow their mums' poo to get the gut bacteria they need to digest plants.

What use are poo and wee?

Caterpillar poo tea is an expensive Chinese tea brewed from the tiny droppings of caterpillars, mixed with tea leaves. The stewed poo is said to soothe the stomach.

Cowpat-throwing contests are popular in the American town of Beaver, Oklahoma. First prize goes to the person who can fling a dried cowpat furthest without breaking it.

Gunpowder was once made from the poo and wee of farm animals. When left to ripen for a year or so, this smelly concoction produces the chemical saltpetre. This makes an explosive mix when added to charcoal and sulphur.

Perfect perfumes need earthy or musky undertones – such as the faint odour of poo. Perfume makers use synthetic versions of the stinky sulphur chemicals in poo.

Camel pellets come out so dry that they make an ideal fuel for desert campfires. In other parts of the world, people also use buffalo and cow dung for cooking and heating.

Most of us **flush the loo** without a backward glance, but not everyone lets their waste go to waste. Since ancient times, people have found all sorts of surprising uses for poo and wee, from **brewing coffee** to **making gunpowder**.

Elephant poo paper is made from the jumbo-sized droppings of elephants. The animals eat so much rough plant matter that their poo resembles the wood pulp that paper is normally made from.

Smell the coffee – civet coffee is a luxury drink made from coffee beans pooed out by animals called civets. Or for a change, try black ivory, which is made from coffee beans in elephant dung.

Wee wash might sound unpleasant, but the ancient Romans used wee to clean their teeth and to wash clothes. Stale wee produces the chemical ammonia – a powerful cleaning agent.

Manure fertilizer is a natural alternative to the chemicals that farmers use to boost the growth of their crops. Alpaca and chicken poo are among the best types of manure.

Dung bricks have been used to build houses for thousands of years and are still used today. They are made from less smelly types of animal poo, such as antelope dung.

Defensive dung

PLAYING *DEAD*

Poo can make a great **defensive weapon**. If an opossum meets a predator, its first line of defence is to snarl angrily. If that fails, the opossum plays dead. It drops to the ground, lets its tongue hang out, and releases a puddle of foul-smelling, greenish **anal fluid**.

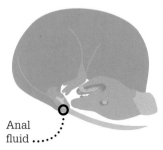

Anal fluid

EGG ESCAPE

Egg

Poo

In Africa's Kalahari desert, trees to nest in are hard to find so the double-banded courser lays its eggs on the ground. To hide them from nosey animals, it puts them among **antelope droppings**, which are just the same size and colour.

STINKY SHIELD

The larvae (maggots) of three-lined potato beetles **smear themselves with poo** laced with poison from the plants they eat. This **faecal shield** protects them from birds.

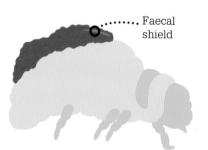

Faecal shield

A TALE OF DEFENCE

Certain South American scorpions escape predators by **shedding their tail.** But this means they also shed their anus, which is at the end of the tail. As a result, they slowly swell up with poo until they **die of constipation**. Even so, they survive long enough to complete their life cycle.

Stinger

Anus

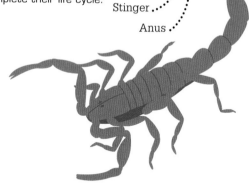

POOP SHOOTERS

Foxes get one in the eye if they bother hoopoe chicks in their nest. When danger threatens, the chicks turn round and shoot a well-aimed **jet of liquid excrement** in the intruder's face. For extra protection, they also smear themselves with an oily secretion that reeks of rotting meat.

Jet of poo

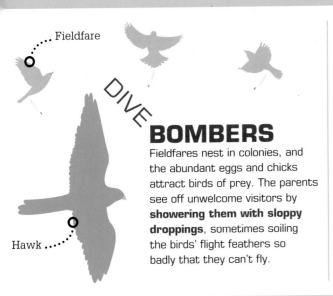

Fieldfare

Hawk

DIVE BOMBERS

Fieldfares nest in colonies, and the abundant eggs and chicks attract birds of prey. The parents see off unwelcome visitors by **showering them with sloppy droppings**, sometimes soiling the birds' flight feathers so badly that they can't fly.

FATAL FART

The larva of the beaded lacewing uses its back passage not for defence but for attack. It lives in termite nests and stuns its termite prey with **toxic fart gases**. One lacewing fart can **paralyse and kill** up to six termites.

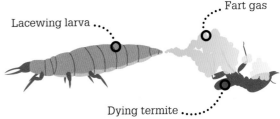

Lacewing larva

Fart gas

Dying termite

SEA OF POO

Whales sometimes resort to fouling the water with a diarrhoea-like discharge when danger threatens. For maximum effect, they whip up the cloud of faeces with their powerful tails, creating a "**poonado**" that puts off all but the most desperate predators.

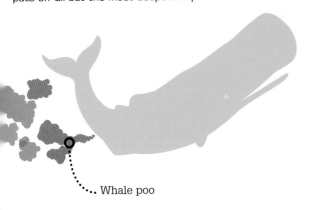

Whale poo

Dried poo forms a hard shield.

The larva bats off attackers with its poo shield.

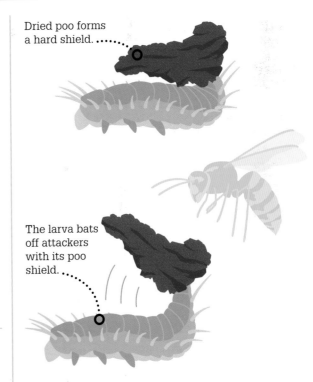

Camouflaged caterpillar

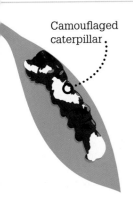

FAKE FAECES

Birds love to eat caterpillars – but not bird poo. The caterpillars of swallowtail butterflies stay safe by **perfectly mimicking** the revolting, slimy shape and colours of a fresh bird dropping oozing down a leaf.

WHACKY TAIL

The **telescoping anus** of the tortoise beetle larva is used to daub droppings on the back of its tail, forming a hard shield of **dried poo**. When ants, wasps, or spiders bother the larva, a powerful flick of the tail bats them way.

How strong is a **dung beetle**?

Gram for gram, the **strongest insect on Earth** is the dung beetle. It uses its strength not just to manoeuvre great balls of dung but also to dig tunnels and fight off rival dung beetles.

Many dung beetles shape dung into balls so that they can roll it away quickly.

CLEAN-UP SQUAD

Dung beetles arrive on fresh poo in minutes by flying towards the smell. They work quickly, racing to hide the dung before other beetles steal it. African dung beetles can clear a heap of elephant poo in under two hours.

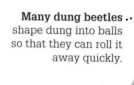

A dung beetle can support a weight up to **1,141 times heavier than** its body.

FAST FACTS

Dung beetles live on every continent except Antarctica, and there are about 10,000 species (types). Most are strong fliers, and many types have beautifully coloured wing-cases.

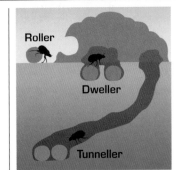

Roller

Dweller

Tunneller

There are three main types of dung beetle.

Rollers make balls of dung, roll them away, and then hide them in a tunnel.
Dwellers make their nests inside a heap of dung.
Tunnellers dig burrows under a pile of dung before hiding the dung inside the burrows.

Muscle power

Scientists measured the strength of dung beetles by gluing cotton threads to them and getting them to haul weights over pulleys. The beetles use their muscle power to bury dung balls before laying eggs in them. The adults don't eat poo directly. Instead, they drink the nutritious liquid that oozes out of fresh poo.

If a human could support 1,141 times their own body weight, they'd be able to hold up 80 tonnes – the weight of six double-decker buses.

Why are wombat poos square?

Millions of animals do sausage-shaped poos, and millions more produce small round pellets. But there's only **one animal** in the world that **poos cubes: the wombat**.

The square poos of wombats are about the size of dice and are easier to stack than round poos.

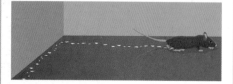

Wombats produce 80–100 cubic poos a night, usually in small heaps of 6–8.

Wombats are marsupials (pouched mammals) and live in Australia. They hide in burrows by day and come out at night to eat grass.

Wombats like to poo in prominent places, such as on logs, rocks, or areas of raised ground. Their droppings serve as territorial markers, telling other wombats that they've visited. Scientists think the poos are square to stop them rolling away and to make them easier to stack.

PHEROMONES

The wee of certain animals contains chemicals called pheromones, which affect the biology of animals that smell them. The wee of male mouse lemurs, for example, contains pheromones that make other males unable to breed.

What's the biggest pile of poo in the world?

Bird and bat poo (guano) can build up in vast piles. A guano mountain known as the **Great Heap** in Peru was 60 m (200 ft) tall, but some piles of bat guano could be even taller.

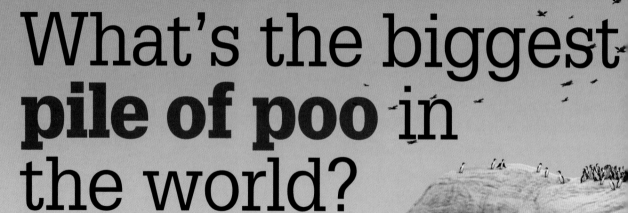

The Leaning Tower of Pisa is 56 m (186 ft) tall.

The **Great Heap** was taller than Italy's Leaning Tower of Pisa.

Seabird droppings built up into a mountain of poo.

It took thousands of years for the Great Heap to build up on North Chincha Island in the Pacific Ocean, but by 1874 it had vanished. The precious poo made the world's finest fertilizer and was mined with pickaxes to be shipped all over the world. It was worth so much money that Peru and Spain went to war over the Chincha Islands – the only war in history that was fought over poo.

FAST FACTS

Animal poo can pile up in surprising places, from sandy beaches to caverns.

It looks like paradise, but the white coral sand of tropical beaches is fish poo. Parrot fish crunch coral reefs with their tough teeth and poo out the gritty remains as fine white sand.

Mounds of guano build up under bat colonies, providing food for a whole ecosystem of cave life. The biggest of these dung heaps may be as much as 100 m (330 ft) tall.

POO PRODUCERS

There's very little nesting material on the rocky and arid Chincha Islands, so seabirds like the guanay cormorant build their nests with the only soft stuff available: poo. Their droppings soon solidify in the dry climate, forming a rock-like crust.

Plant-eating animals have a longer digestive system than meat eaters because plants are much harder to digest than meat. Some plant eaters, such as horses, eat masses of food but digest it poorly and poo out piles of half-digested straw. Others, such as cows, digest food slowly and carefully, which requires very long intestines. If a cow's intestines weren't coiled up, its body would be about 50 m (160 ft) long.

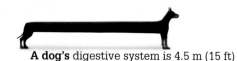

A dog's digestive system is 4.5 m (15 ft) long – five times longer than its body.

A lion's digestive system is 6 m (20 ft) long – three times longer than its body.

A horse's digestive system is 21 m (69 ft) long – ten times longer than its body.

A sheep's digestive system is 25 m (82 ft) long – 19 times longer than its body.

An elephant's digestive system is 35 m (115 ft) long – seven times longer than its body.

FAST FACTS

How quickly animals can digest food and turn a meal into a poo varies a great deal. Food passes through a songbird's body in under an hour, helping it keep its weight down and fly more easily. In contrast, a large snake can take over a year to fully digest a large meal after swallowing its victim whole.

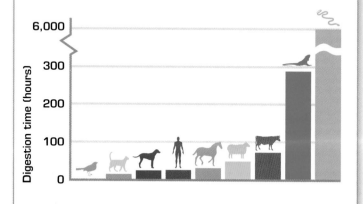

How **far** does **food travel**?

Food goes on a **long journey** as it passes through an animal's body, slowly turning into poo. The trip from mouth to anus goes through the coiled tubes of the **digestive system**, which are packed inside the animal's belly.

The human digestive system is 6.5 m (21 ft) long – nearly four times greater than an average adult's height.

A cow's digestive system is **20 times longer** than its body.

A cow's digestive system is 50 m (164 ft) long. It takes 3 days for food to pass through.

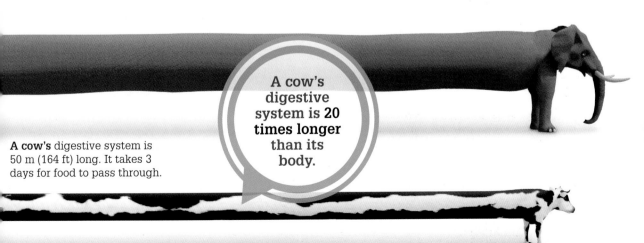

How much methane gas do cows fart?

As they digest food, cows and other farm animals produce the gas methane – one of the most **powerful greenhouse gases** known. Every year, cows release around 54 million tonnes of methane.

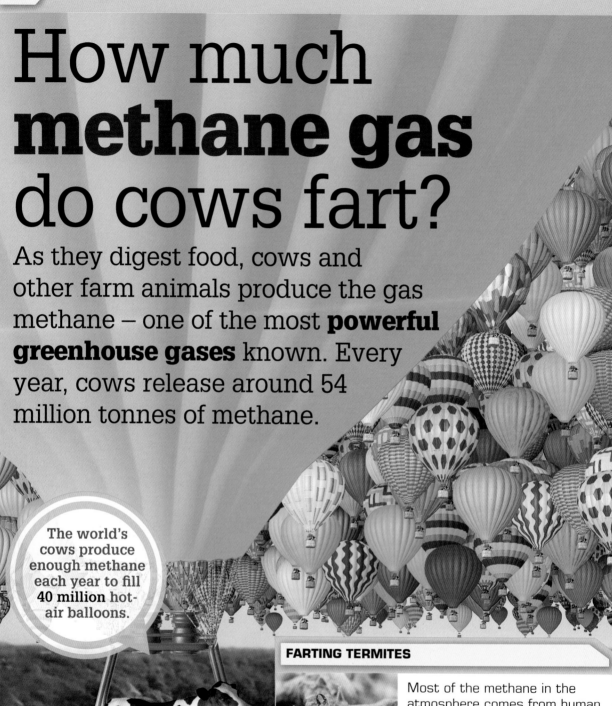

The world's cows produce enough methane each year to fill **40 million** hot-air balloons.

FARTING TERMITES

Most of the methane in the atmosphere comes from human activities, but there are natural sources too. Termites fart out 11 million tonnes of methane a year, made by wood-digesting microbes in their gut.

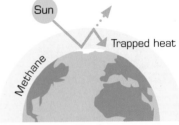

Sun

Trapped heat

Methane

Earth

Methane is a greenhouse gas, which means it traps heat in Earth's atmosphere, causing global warming. Methane traps 28 times as much heat as carbon dioxide, the best known greenhouse gas.

Scientists estimate that producing 1 kg (2.2 lbs) of beef does as much damage to Earth's atmosphere (through greenhouse gas emissions) as driving a car for 260 km (160 miles).

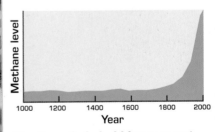

Methane level

1000   1200   1400   1600   1800   2000
Year

Studies of air bubbles trapped in ancient glaciers reveal that atmospheric methane levels have risen steeply in recent years. The methane comes not just from cattle farming but also from rice farms, rotting landfill, and gas leaks from fossil fuel industries.

Plant-eating animals have methane-producing microorganisms in their stomachs or intestines to help them digest plants. A cow can release up to 300 litres (630 pints) of methane a day. Only a small amount escapes in farts – most is belched out of the mouth.

What's the biggest fossil poo?

Poo, whether human or animal, doesn't normally last long after it hits the ground as tiny organisms quickly devour it. However, a few rare dollops last long enough to turn into **fossil poos – coprolites**.

The world's longest claimed coprolite is an **eye-watering 102 cm (40 in)** in length.

The longest claimed coprolite is 6 million years old and was found in the remains of a prehistoric swamp in Washington State, USA. Exactly what kind of animal produced this giant poo is a mystery. Some scientists suspect it might be a cast of a dead animal's intestine. Others think it might not be a fossil poo at all but just a squiggly mass of clay that oozed out of a rotting log. The record-breaking specimen sold at auction in 2014 for $10,370.

⊞ FAST FACTS

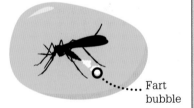

Fart
bubble

The largest coprolite of a meat-eating dinosaur is a 66-million-year-old *Tyrannosaurus* poo, measuring 44 cm (17 in) long. It was found in Canada in 1998. Nearly half the fossil consists of ground-up bone from a smaller dinosaur the predator ate.

The world's oldest farts have been found as bubbles of gas trapped with insects in amber (fossilized tree sap). These bubbles probably erupted after the insects died. Scientists have found fossilized farts of cockroaches, termites, midges, beetles, and ants.

The coprolite was carefully reconstructed from broken fragments.

GIANT SLOTH COPROLITE

Some of the largest collections of coprolites come from caves in the Grand Canyon, USA. About 20,000 years ago, the caves were used as latrines (communal toilets) by prehistoric mammals called giant sloths. Their fossilized dung now forms heaps up to 6 m (20 ft) deep.

Actual size!

What's the biggest poo parasite?

Parasites are organisms that live in or on our bodies, feeding on us. The **largest human parasite** is the tapeworm. It lives in our intestines and spreads by laying eggs in poo.

Mature segments drop off the end of the tail and crawl away to escape in poo. If the poo is washed into a river or ocean, fish eat the worm's eggs and become infected.

> A tapeworm can grow to 9 m (30 ft) long in a person's body.

Blue whale

Whale tapeworm

The blue whale is the world's largest animal, but the whale tapeworm, which lives inside it, is just as long. A whale tapeworm can grow to 35 m (115 ft) long.

TAPEWORM HEAD

Many kinds of tapeworm have hooks or suckers on the head so they can anchor themselves firmly to the inside wall of our small intestine. A tapeworm has no eyes, mouth, or stomach. It feeds by absorbing the food that we have already digested.

The longest tapeworms of all are fish tapeworms – so-called because we get them by eating undercooked fish. A fish tapeworm's body is divided into as many as 3,000 segments. New segments develop near the worm's head. As they grow, the segments move to the tail and produce eggs. A fish tapeworm can live for 20 years and can produce 1 million eggs a day.

Each segment has male and female parts and can produce thousands of eggs, which are stored inside it.

Record breakers

PONGIEST POO

Which animal makes the **pongiest poo**? There are plenty of contenders, from the sickening, fishy poo of whales to the **overpowering stench** of fox poo. But perhaps the pongiest poo — to any animal species — is its own. We find our own poo smellier and more repulsive than animal poo because human poo is more likely to carry germs that can give us diseases.

GOLD FLUSH

The world's **most expensive toilet** is in the showroom of the Hang Fung jewellery store in Hong Kong. Crafted out of **24 carat solid gold**, it's worth about **£2.4 million**. Even the floor and toilet brush are made of gold. But don't think you can spend a penny here — the golden throne is never used.

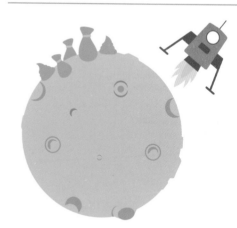

PRICIEST HUMAN POO

Start saving! The **most expensive human poo** is worth **£30,000**. The "Lloyds Bank coprolite" was deposited in York, England, around 1,200 years ago by a Viking who was infested with parasitic worms. It measures a whopping **20 cm (8 in) long**.

FARTHEST FAECES

The Universe is full of space debris, but not all of it comes from meteorite collisions. Apollo astronauts left a total of **96 faecal bags** on various parts of the Moon. They are officially the most distant dumps from planet Earth.

BIGGEST POO
STAIN

Penguins are the only animals whose poo stains are so big they **are visible from space**. Adélie and emperor penguins live in vast colonies that stain the pure white snow of Antarctica pink or grey with droppings. Scientists use satellite images of the poo stains to work out how many penguins live in each colony.

F O U L E S T   F A R T S

With a few exceptions, such as sloths, all large animals break wind. But the trophy for foulest farts should probably go to sea lions, which zookeepers say can clear a crowd of visitors faster than any other animal — thanks to **deadly blasts** that stink of rotten fish and squid.

B E S T   P O O P
SHOOTER

For its size, the skipper butterfly caterpillar of North America can **shoot poo further** than any other animal. Its ballistic bottom has a kind of latch that holds emerging pellets in place while pressure builds up. Lifting the latch fires droppings 1.5 m (5 ft) away, which is more than **38 times the caterpillar's length**. That's like a human firing a poo across a football field.

Take cover if you ever come across a male hippopotamus at toilet time. When nature calls, this animal spins its muscular tail like a propeller to **splatter excrement** everywhere — much like poo hitting a fan. **Flinging dung** is important to male hippos because the females find it attractive.

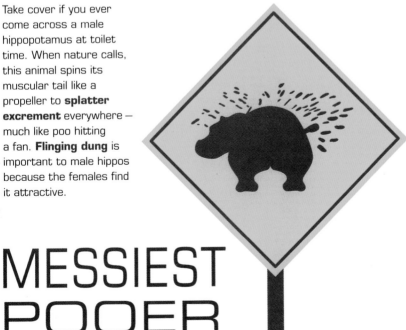

MESSIEST
POOER

PRICIEST
ANIMAL POO

The most highly prized animal poo belongs to the sperm whale and goes for **£50,000 per 1.5 kg (3lb)**. Perfume-makers have a whale of a time using the waxy waste known as ambergris as a main ingredient for many fragrances and colognes. The price is pushed up both for its sweet smell and the way it sticks to the skin.

INDEX

ACKNOWLEDGEMENTS

Dorling Kindersley would like to thank the following people for scientific consultation: Roberto Berardi of the European Tissue Symposium; Dr. Adrian P. Hunt; Professor Ron Milo and Ron Sender at the Weizmann Institute, Israel; Savetheelephants.org. The publisher would also like to thank Shaila Brown for editorial help; Jacqui Swan for design help; Katie John for proofreading; and Helen Peters for indexing.

The publisher would like to thank the following for their kind permission to reproduce their photographs:

(Key: a-above; b-below/bottom; c-centre; f-far; l-left; r-right; t-top)

4–5 iStockphoto.com: ikopylov (c). **7 Science Photo Library:** Gastrolab (ca); David M. Martin, MD (clb); David Musher (cb). **9 Science Photo Library:** Steve Gschmeissner (crb); SCIMAT (cra, cr). **10 Science Photo Library:** Biozentrum, University Of Basel (clb). **17 Alamy Stock Photo:** Science History Images (cra). **18 Alamy Stock Photo:** Rick & Nora Bowers (clb). **18–19 Alamy Stock Photo:** Dennis MacDonald. **21 Alamy Stock Photo:** Jean Luc Brouard / robertharding (bc). **25 Getty Images:** Adrian Dennis / AFP (cb). **28 Alamy Stock Photo:** Michael Dietrich / imageBROKER (cl). **30 Alamy Stock Photo:** NG Images (clb). **36 Alamy Stock Photo:** Joost Adriaanse (bl). **38 123RF.com:** Aleksandar Kitanovic (clb). **Alamy Stock Photo:** Rosanne Tackaberry (cr). **38–39 Dreamstime.com:** Janazak (c).

39 Dreamstime.com: Crystal Craig / Crystalcraig (bl). **40 naturepl.com:** Solvin Zankl (cl). **42 Alamy Stock Photo:** Paul Riccardi (br). **Dorling Kindersley:** Natural History Museum, London (ca). **43 Alamy Stock Photo:** National Geographic Image Collection (ca). **Dreamstime.com:** Anankkml (crb). **46 Alamy Stock Photo:** Images of Africa Photobank (cl). **49 FLPA:** Chien Lee / Minden Pictures (crb). **51 FLPA:** E.J. Peiker / Minden Pictures (crb). **54 123RF.com:** Mr. Smith Chetanachan / smuay (bc). **57 National Museum of Natural History, Smithsonian Institution:** Photo courtesy Chip Clark (crb). **59 Alamy Stock Photo:** Science Photo Library (cr).

All other images © Dorling Kindersley
For further information see: www.dkimages.com